CAROLINA PANTHERS

Amy Sawyer

LET'S READ
AV²
BY WEIGL™
ADDED VALUE • AUDIO VISUAL

AV² provides enriched content that supplements and complements this book. Weigl's AV² books strive to create inspired learning and engage young minds in a total learning experience.

Your AV² Media Enhanced books come alive with...

Audio
Listen to sections of the book read aloud.

Video
Watch informative video clips.

Embedded Weblinks
Gain additional information for research.

Try This!
Complete activities and hands-on experiments.

Key Words
Study vocabulary, and complete a matching word activity.

Quizzes
Test your knowledge.

Slide Show
View images and captions, and prepare a presentation.

...and much, much more!

Go to www.av2books.com, and enter this book's unique code.

BOOK CODE

M 8 4 4 5 8 7

AV² by Weigl brings you media enhanced books that support active learning.

Published by AV² by Weigl
350 5th Avenue, 59th Floor
New York, NY 10118

Website: www.av2books.com

Library of Congress Control Number: 2017930537

ISBN 978-1-4896-5487-8 (hardcover)
ISBN 978-1-4896-5489-2 (multi-user eBook)

Printed in the United States of America in Brainerd, Minnesota
1 2 3 4 5 6 7 8 9 0 21 20 19 18 17

032017
020317

Editor: Katie Gillespie
Art Director: Terry Paulhus

Weigl acknowledges Getty Images and iStock as the primary image suppliers for this title.

My First NFL Book

CAROLINA PANTHERS

CONTENTS

Team History

The Carolina Panthers joined the NFL in 1993. They were the first new team in 17 years. Jerry Richardson is the founder and owner. The Panthers represent both North Carolina and South Carolina. They are the only NFL team to play for two states.

The Panthers sold 41,632 lifetime seats the first day they went on sale.

The Stadium

The Panthers play at Bank of America Stadium. It opened in 1996. There are 75,419 seats. Bank of America Stadium is one of only two stadiums that has the NFL logo in the middle of the field instead of the team logo.

Bank of America Stadium in Charlotte, North Carolina, is painted blue and black to match the team colors.

Team Spirit

Sir Purr is the Panthers' mascot. His jersey number is 00. Sir Purr leads the team onto the field at the start of every game. He hugs Panthers fans and players. Sir Purr's family members sometimes join him at games.

Sir Purr visits schools to help kids study for tests.

The Jerseys

The Panthers have three different jerseys. The first is black, the second is white, and the third is blue. The Panthers wear their blue jerseys two times a year. The NFL has a rule that teams can only wear a third uniform style twice each season.

11

The Helmet

The Panthers' helmets are silver. They have the team logo on each side. The logo is a roaring black panther. Two black stripes go down the middle and then curl behind the panther's head.

Face masks have been part of every NFL helmet since 1962.

14

The Coach

Ron Rivera was hired as the head coach of the Panthers in 2011. He worked as a coach for three other NFL teams before joining the Panthers. He is the third Latino head coach in NFL history. Rivera has been named the NFL Coach of the Year twice with the Panthers.

Player Positions

The offense works together to move the ball and score. Wide receivers are some of the fastest players. Their job is to catch passes from the quarterback. Passes can be short or long.

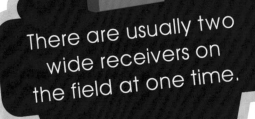

2

There are usually two wide receivers on the field at one time.

Star Player

Cam Newton is the Panthers' quarterback. He set an NFL record for the most passing yards by a rookie. A rookie is a person who is playing his first season. Newton also set an NFL record for the most rushing touchdowns by a quarterback. This means he ran the ball into the end zone himself.

Steve Smith was a wide receiver for the Panthers from 2001 to 2013. He has the team record for most yards catching the ball. Smith scored 454 points for the team. This is the second most in team history. He set another team record by catching the ball at least once in 71 straight games.

Team Records

Sam Mills was the first player to join the Panthers Hall of Honor. This is the team's version of the Hall of Fame. He made 385 tackles as a linebacker. John Kasay was a Panthers' kicker. He is the team's all-time leading scorer. He scored 1,482 points. The Panthers had a 17–2 record in 2015. This is the best record the team has ever had.

17–2
Best Season Record

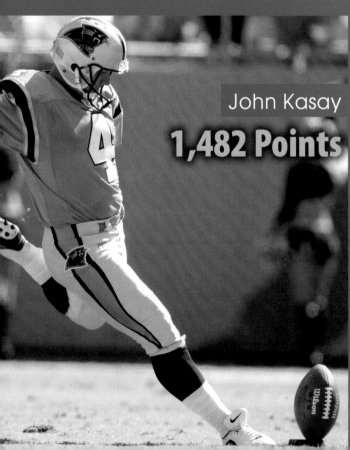

John Kasay

1,482 Points

Sam Mills

385 Tackles

By the Numbers

The Panthers have a **30**-person drumline called PurrCussion that plays at each game.

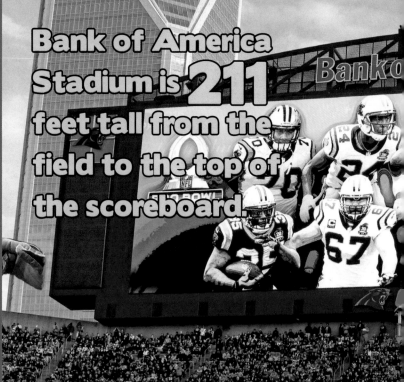

Bank of America Stadium is **211** feet tall from the field to the top of the scoreboard.

The Panthers' first win was **26–15** against the New York Jets on **October 15, 1995.**

The Panthers were the **29**th team to join the NFL.

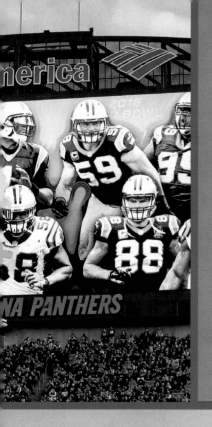

The Panthers won
7 games
in their first season.

This set an NFL record for most wins in the first season by a new team.

Running back DeAngelo Williams set a team record by running with the ball for
210 yards
in **one game.**

Quiz

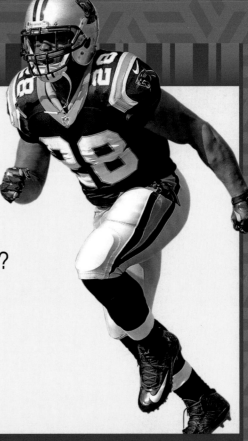

1. When did Bank of America Stadium open?

2. Who is the Panthers' mascot?

3. How many times per season can the Panthers wear their blue jerseys?

4. How many points did Steve Smith score for the team?

5. What was the Panthers' record in 2015?

Check out www.av2books.com for activities, videos, audio clips, and more!

MEDIA ENHANCED BOOKS
AV2 BY WEIGL™
ADDED VALUE · AUDIO VISUAL

1 Go to www.av2books.com.

2 Enter book code. M844587

3 Fuel your imagination online!

www.av2books.com